A Lost Stranger

Echoes from a Ghost in the Crowd

Shatanik Bhar

Made with ❤ on the BookLeaf Publishing Platform
www.bookleafpub.in
www.bookleafpub.com

Dedication

To my sister, who carries the weight of guilt for leaving me behind- if only she knew she's the one I look up to, and the one I'm most proud of in our family.

And to my love, who saw me not as broken, but as becoming — who loved me when I couldn't love myself, with eyes that held the admiration I could never find within, and a strength that carried me when I had none of my own.

Preface

These poems are born from countless sleepless nights—each verse a reflection of emotions too heavy to keep inside. They are the quiet conversations I never had, the unsent letters, the words I whispered into the darkness when no one was listening. This is not just a collection of words—it's a journey through the depths of feeling lost, aching for meaning, and learning to navigate the silent spaces in between.

With each page turned, you'll witness the slow unravelling and rebuilding of a soul—one that longed to belong, to be seen, to be understood. These poems trace the path of someone who has wandered through doubt and desire, who has fallen apart and stitched themselves back together using only fragments of hope and truth.

So as you journey through this book, may you feel seen in the silences, held in the heartbreaks, and guided by the light tucked between each line. These poems are not answers—they are offerings. Pieces of soul left behind like breadcrumbs for anyone wandering, wondering, or waiting to feel whole again.

If you've ever felt like a ghost in a world too loud, like a whisper in a storm, know this: you are not alone. Your pain is valid. Your softness is sacred. And your story—no matter how quiet—is worth telling.

A Lost Stranger is more than my voice; it is a sanctuary for all the unspoken things we carry. A space to rest. A place to remember who you are, and what you're becoming.

And perhaps, if you've ever felt like a stranger in this world—unseen in a crowd, unheard in conversation, uncertain in your own skin—this book was always meant to find you.

Acknowledgements

This book would not exist without the love, support, and quiet strength of the people who stood by me through every storm and silence.

To my parents—thank you for raising me. I know we've always been a complicated family and have had our fair share of disagreements and fights. But I also know you did the best you could—after all, it's your first time parenting in this world, too. I know parents are often compared to gods, but I've always seen you as humans—vulnerable, imperfect, and learning as you go. And that, to me, is just as admirable.

To my sister, whom I've recently begun to open up to—there's comfort in knowing someone who has lived through the same walls and experiences. Even though Mom thinks we just laugh and joke about everything, I know that even when we cry, we'll always have each other. You've always been, and will always be, my anchor.

To my friends—thank you for accepting me as I am. I tend to distance myself at times, struggle to communicate, and find it hard to ask for help. But through true friendships (and even the difficult ones), I've learned that the ones who truly want to stay in your life, will. Time and space can never keep them away for long. And when we meet, no matter how much time has passed, we always pick up right where we left off.

To my love—thank you for making me believe there's still goodness left in this world. For reigniting the spark in me and gently guiding me out of the darkness I once called home. I never knew I had so much love in me until I gave it to you. These poems weren't all written with you in mind, but somehow, every word and every line eventually led me to you. Thank you for loving me—and even the parts I try to hide. You are, without a doubt, the best thing that has ever happened to me.

To every soul who ever felt out of place, unseen, or unheard—this book is for you. You've helped me find my voice by echoing back the parts of myself I once tried to hide.

I carry your love, your words, and your presence in every page—this book is as much yours as it is mine.

1. The End

People fear death.
I fear living,
While everything inside you is dead.
All the dreams that I painted,
Turned black and white in my head.

How could I be happy,
Knowing what happiness costs?
Knowing that everything I've loved
Are the things that I've lost.

They say-
"What doesn't kill you,
Makes you stronger."
But I don't want to be strong anymore
All I want is to be found,
Like empty shells on a seashore.

Maybe I'm too broken to be fixed,
Apologizing for things that weren't my fault.
And time can heal, but this won't-
Opening wounds just to pour salt.

2. Afterlife

One day,
I never woke up.
And that was the day
I was loved the most.
Shedding tears over a corpse,
I saw mortals speaking to a ghost.

Even strangers came dressed as friends
And people I'd never known.
Hoping they had shown up,
While I was dying all alone.

Old photos were hung,
And candles lit in my memory.
Strangers circled to share my story,
But all they did was mumble the summary.

Now that there's no one to blame,
I bet they'll be cursing the knife.
Knowing that slitting my throat
Didn't end my life.

It had already ended
The day I felt so numb inside.
And nobody cared to love me then,
When I was fucking alive!

3. Oxymoron

I've seen people live,
While everything's dead inside.
Getting high to have fun,
Or is it the pain they're trying to hide?

And that one guy,
Trying to make everyone laugh,
Cries himself to sleep at night.
Wonder why we always end up losing,
If we try to hold on too tight.
And the ones who believed
"Things would get better"
Are now wrapped in white.
Was it the darkness that killed them
Or the hope for light?

The ones who are supposed to love us,
Hurt us the most.
While the world pictures us
From our happy Instagram posts.
And it's sad yet true
How beautifully irony resides
In everything that we do.

Maybe all good things
Don't hold value alone.
So, we put them next to bad ones,
Creating a perfect oxymoron.

4. Crimson Rain

Hot poker in my chest,
Just to feel the pain.
Peel my skin
To reveal those veins.

Bandages on wounds,
Won't hide bloodstains.
So, the world turns red
When I stand in the rain.

Saw my castle crumble down,
Dancing with the hurricane.
There's nothing I could do,
Tied up in chains.

So, I shot myself,
Bullets deep in my brain.
No matter what people say,
They might think I'm insane.
But what's the point of living,
When my life's in vain?

5. Purgatory

Sometimes, I wonder-

Why we cry
Whilst everyone around us
Celebrates our birth.

Then again,
Maybe we're angels
Weighted by our sins,
Lost our wings,
As we fell
Down to Earth.

6. Ephemeral

Losing has always been a part of us-
From losing paper planes
That were never found,
To losing friends
Who never stuck around.

Remember that balloon?
That you let go at the fair.
Or the plant that died?
Even after all that care.

Tell me, did you cry
When your mom left you at school?
'Cause I cried too.
And did you lie
When you wiped your tears
Saying *"It's fine"*?
'Cause I lied too.

Losing has always been a part of us-
Like footprints in the sand
Before you know it, they're gone,
All washed away into even land.

7. Endorphins

I wish chemicals were only found in labs
Instead of our heads-
So we could pour them down the drain
And not put a gun to our mouths
To blow out our brains.

But how sad would it be
To feel nothing—to go numb?
To not even laugh at ourselves
Doing something so dumb.

So, suck it up with a smile,
Fuck it up and disappear for a while.
Bare your wounds and let them bruise-
'Cause the more you hold in
The more you lose.

8. Inkbound

Not always my pen speaks feelings.
Not always does the paper oozes blue.
Poetry is an art of emotions,
Not just rhyming words that aren't even true.

And for me,
Poetry resides within you,
Spilling syllables every time you breathe-
A hymn wrapped in human skin,
Hiding the essence of life underneath.

So, I write you down
To keep you safe.
Loving you through these pages,
Is all that I can do.
And like every other thought crossing my mind,
I don't want to lose you too.

So, don't ask me,
Whom I write those poems for.
There's nothing you don't already know.
Scattered in those words lie
Pieces of you that I can't let go.

9. Where Hearts Go

Where do broken hearts go?
Maybe back to the place
Where they truely belong-
Like a flock of birds
Returning after a day so long.

Or perhaps,
They hide themselves in gallery
Scrolled through every night
Until they fall asleep.
Sad how people we love
Leave wounds so deep.

Maybe they're lost
Somewhere in the old chats.
The ones they read
To find where it all went wrong—
Traveling back in time,
When it all started with a song.

I guess,
We'll never know,
Where these broken hearts go.
What if these feelings never left?
Like a fear we'll never overcome.
Constantly reminding us who we are,
And what we're yet to become.

10. Aishiteru

She doesn't reside in poems;
Poetry lives within her.
Flowing through her veins,
In the brightest possible colour.

Spilling through her eyes,
As she looks at the moon.
Staring at the stars, as if
She'll be joining them soon.

11. In Dawn's Wake

This morning,
I saw her smile as she looked at me,
A thousand memories flashed in my mind-
Of who we are, and what we're meant to be.

There were words left untold
The ones I wish I had said
Instead, I just smiled back
And nodded my head.

And now,
I'm left with nothing but her,
Noticing everything that she did.
Laughing at her own jokes
Only revealed the pain she hid.

And she hid it well.
Whatever she did, she did it well-
Or at least she tried.
Putting on a happy face,
Right after the moment she cried.

She's too beautiful to be this broken
With hair curling around her face.
And the way she tucks it behind her ear
Makes the simplest of things find grace.

She carries galaxies in her eyes,
And a universe we don't belong in.
Even the sunshine is blessed
When it falls on her skin.

And the sound of her voice cracking
Feels like dawn breaking-
The silence of night,
Pouring love into everything she touches,
Filling the darkness with light.

12. Burning Moths

If you love someone,
You're going to lose them—
Maybe one way or another,
Someday or the other.

And what stays is the pain,
Reminding you in the pouring rain
Of the paradise we were meant to find.
We had it all, and we lost it all,
With our futures left behind.

This isn't love, darling,
This is war—
A battle between two hearts set afar.
And when they come together, they collide—
Two moths drawn to a flame,
 Just before they died.

13. Colosseum

I fell in love with a poet
Not the usual kind,
But with someone
You'd rarely find.

Words couldn't do her justice,
So she wrote in scars instead,
Etching grief and fear-
A perfect rhyme from toe to head.
She doesn't create art; she is art,
Her poetry like the ruins of the Colosseum-
Not for everyone to witness,
But meant to be preserved in a museum.

14. Saved As Draft

Hope, I loved you
Knowing how to end it.
Instead, wrote *"I love you"*
Just to unsend it.

And all those backspaces
Hold more secrets
Than I ever told you.
Photos being the only place
Where I could still hold you.

But don't you worry,
These feelings won't last forever,
And neither will I.
So I lay awake every night,
Because I can sleep when I die.

15. Beneath The Surface

Take care of her.
You have no idea
What she has been through.
You only see the tip of the iceberg,
In her ocean, deep blue.

Trust me,
She needs you far more
Than you'll ever need her.
Yet all you do is break
The pieces she gathers.

But she doesn't need saving.
Just wants to be understood,
As she fights her own battle
Between evil and good.

16. Loving Can Hurt

Loving can hurt sometimes.
 You may never get back what you pay,
But it'll all come back to you
In most unexpected ways.

Even on the bad days
You decide to stay-
Awake all night,
Just to make them feel okay.

And before bed, you pray
That it's still the two of you
At the end of the day.
That your hearts, painted in shades of grey,
Might light up like the summer of May.

Loving can hurt sometimes,
But it's worth it, they say-
Finding something to hold onto,
You don't just throw it away.

17. 4 letters

Just because you made them happy
Doesn't mean you can make them sad.
Just because you've suffered
Doesn't allow you to treat them bad.
Just because things could be different
Doesn't mean they would've been better.
And just because you feel drawn to them
Doesn't mean you can put it in four letters.

18. Philophobia

Why do I fear love, you ask?
After all, it was the reason for my happiness
But what good is joy
If it leaves you sad?
Like all good things in life
That turned out to be bad.

Why do I fear love, you ask?
Because it gave me hope-
A dream too far from true
Yet I held onto that idea, 'cause
That's the closest I can get to you.

And you ask,
Why do I fear love?
Because I know what comes next-
Watching things change
From phone calls to texts,
To nothing at all
'Cause a heart that's broken
Is a heart that falls.

19. 3 AM

It's 3 am, and I'm lying still,
Neither alcohol nor pills,
But an old familiar ache in my chest,
A quiet reminder as I rest.

I turn my head, switch sides,
 Pull the blanket up to hide
 Memories slipping from my eyes
 Of a beautiful world,
 Of pretty white lies-
That my mind had once created
To escape the reality that I hated.

A world where we're meant to be,
A world as delicate as sand.
The tighter I try to hold it,
The quicker it slips out of my hand

20. Grand Gestures

Love isn't about grand gestures,
Yet people fail to understand.
It's like crossing a road together,
Holding hands,
Keeping her on the other side of traffic
While you stand.

It's in dropping her home
After a long day out,
Or educating her on something
She doesn't know about.

It's in defending her name
When she's not around,
Or calling her after a bad day,
To make sure she's safe and sound.

21. Little Things

Why is it always the smallest of details
That I notice about you?
Like the way you tuck your hair
Behind your ear,
Or the fact that your hand turns cold
When speaking of things you fear.

The way your smile widens
When you talk about your dreams
Or how a single glance
Tells me exactly what you mean.

The way you like your coffee hot
On a rainy day,
Or how you sacrifice your happiness
Worrying what people would say.

But most importantly,
The way you look at things-
Always grateful for today, and
Hopeful about what tomorrow brings.

22. Letters Past Twelve

I've been writing a lot these days,
 Wishing it were for myself—
 But if it was,
 I wouldn't be scribbling letters past twelve.

I could write a book about you,
If that brings a smile to your face.
Building bridges with these phrases,
Just to reach my happy place.

Maybe someday,
All this makes sense.
When these pages I flip
Turn into past tense.

And maybe that day
I'll string those words together,
And write you a song.
Just promise that you'll stay,
And be there to sing along.

23. Almost Mine

Why do you look
Like everything I've known
And lost, at the same time?
But not every beautiful poem
Is one that rhymes.

Why do you look
Like something I've prayed for
All these fucking years?
And the eyes that once dreamt,
Are now filled with tears.

Why do you look
Like something that can't be mine?
An angel wrapped in human skin,
Sent from the heavens above.
Funny how the things we can't have
Are the only ones we love.

24. Under The Same Sky

It's been a long time
Since we last met.
Even the skies cried that day,
Bleeding shades of violet.

And it's scary-
How happy we were
The last time we saw each other.
And how a moment we live in,
Can turn out to be our last together.

But I loved you then,
And I love you now.
And the distance between us,
Brought us closer somehow.

So the next time we meet,
Maybe I'll love you a little more-
While you look me in the eye.
But until then, darling
At least we're under the same sky.

25. How Would You Feel

I never had you in first place,
So why do I fear losing you?
7 billion people on this planet,
So why do I keep choosing you?

Maybe it's better if you leave me-
'Cause that's what they always do.
Else, how would you feel
If I said that I love you?

26. Elysian

I hope your 3a.m. water
Tastes like heaven.
Hope light enters your room
A little past seven.

Hope your morning shower
Washes away your sins.
Hope your mirror doesn't remind you
Of all the dark places you've been.

Hope you tie your hair
Only if its dry enough to.
Hope the perfume you spray
Smells as good as you.

Hope that dress you wear
Compliments your smile.
Hope those earrings your mother gifted
Never go out of style.

Hope you lock the door
Check it twice before you leave.
Hope reality is nothing less
Than what you believe.

27. Heaven Can Wait

I love you,
In a way that no one else could.
I care for you,
The way everyone else should.

I long for you,
Like the sun longs for the moon-
Dying every night
Just to see you rise,
Patiently waiting for you
To light up my dark blue skies.

I praise you,
Keeping you safe in my prayers.
And if someday God decides
To take you back,
I'll meet you up there.

28. Epitaph

Would you ever look at me
The way I look at you?
Like the answers to all my prayers
Lies in the mere presence of you.

And would you ever
Say my name, the way I do?
Sanctifying each syllable,
With the mere mention of you.

And would you ever be
The end of my story,
The way I long for you to be?
Death that comes by your side,
Is the only end I ever wish to see.

29. Restless Reassurances

I could be boring sometimes-
I mean, what more do you expect?
Asking the same questions again,
With no different answers, I suspect.

Still curious about your day,
When it's always been the same.
Getting on your nerves until
It makes you go insane.

I could be hard sometimes,
But i know we'll make it through
Cuz what i fear more than death
Is living without you.

30. Gravity

You're not the center of the universe,
Only my world revolves around you.
Wished upon every shooting star
Until I finally found you.

And now that you're here,
I can't get enough of you.
Can feel it when I'm near,
But still so far away from you.

Could it be that our stars didn't align?
Or should we take it as a sign?
But you're not the center of the universe,
It's just my world
That revolves around you.
How could I escape your gravity
When everything pulls me back to you.

31. Unloving You

I fell in love with a girl
 I wasn't looking for.
Don't know if the world deserves her,
But she deserves everything, and more.

Even on her bad days,
She lights up the room.
Waters dead flowers, as if
One day she'll make them bloom.

Scared of ruining things,
Even when she's done nothing wrong.
Could stare truth in the eyes,
And still, let the lies play along.

She's no angel, not even close
But nothing less than a miracle,
How from the ashes she rose.

I fell in love with this girl
I wasn't looking for.
But if happy-ever-afters exist,
She'll be there for sure.

32. Things You Never Saw

I really hope you'd see it-
Why can't you see it?
How my days begin with your thought
And end with your wait.
And often, how much I love you,
Is the only thing that I hate.

Still, every now and then,
I hope you'd see it.
And appreciate things while they last,
'Cause it'll be over before you know it,
Turning us into strangers from the past.

33. Hiraeth

I had you-
Almost.
Almost found a perfect ending,
An ending too good to be true.
But good things come to an end,
And so did my time with you.

I lost you-
Almost.
Almost let you go,
But my feelings said otherwise.
Intertwined inexplicably,
Holding onto you for dear life.

Because I don't want this love
To haunt us even when we're ghosts.
Never enough, but at least I had you-
Almost.

34. Wabi-Sabi

I fell in love with a girl
 I wasn't looking for.
Don't know if the world deserves her,
But she deserves everything, and more.

Even on her bad days,
She lights up the room.
Waters dead flowers, as if
One day she'll make them bloom.

Scared of ruining things,
Even when she's done nothing wrong.
Could stare truth in the eyes,
And still, let the lies play along.

She's no angel, not even close
But nothing less than a miracle,
How from the ashes she rose.

I fell in love with this girl
I wasn't looking for.
But if happy-ever-afters exist,
She'll be there for sure.

35. The String Of Fate

Not every story gets a fairytale beginning.
Ours started right when it was about to end-
Until we realized,
There's no end to this... is there?

'Cause every time we parted ways,
We ran in circles, just to end up
Together again- like a loop
Repeating itself endlessly through
Turn of events, intertwined inexplicably
With the string of fate, making us
Dance around like puppets.

Although, I don't believe in
The idea of 'meant to be',
But you're still the best thing
That ever happened to me.

In health and in sickness,
In strength and in weakness,
The love that binds us together
Shall spread its wings and fight our demons
At times when we can't.

36. Fragile

The world doesn't deserve you
Maybe, neither do I.
But the world still hurts you,
And all I do is try

To be the reason for my happiness,
To be the reason for your smile,
To be the reason you live
Every once in a while.

Fragile things aren't meant to break;
They're meant to be protected-
From the careless hands,
And the pain that they've inflicted

I can't let you break again,
'Cause I know it'll break me too.
So, when death comes for you,
I'll greet it with open arms
And say, *"Take me too."*

37. I Love You Not

I never said
I like you,
But I'm jealous of the sunlight
That kisses your face every morning,
Just to wake you up on time.
I didn't even say I need you-
So why does it feel like a crime?

I never said I love you
And I don't think I ever would.
Lost are the ones I've loved,
And losing you too
Is something I never could.

38. As Long As You're Happy

Wish I could leave you
All by yourself in this cruel world,
But it would be a sin.
The fear that you'll lose
Whatever little is left in you,
Always crawls under my skin.

And I can't let that happen, can I?
Your pain will be the death of me.
I love you enough for the both of us-
You've put your faith in me,
And I'll keep my faith in God,
As long as you're happy.

39. Caelestis

She has nothing to prove
Her existence is proof itself-
That light can reach
Even the darkest of places,
And flowers can bloom
From the deepest of crevices.
And if any good is left here,
She's the half of it-
Being the missing piece
That doesn't seem to fit.

Although she deserves the world
The world doesn't deserve her back.
So my prayers would guide her home,
Even if she loses her track.

40. If The World Is Ending

The world is ending
So I'd better let you know-
If I had you,
I'd never let you go.

I know it's a bit cliché,
Promising forever so casually.
But the point is,
I don't like people that usually.

And the ones I do
Don't like me back
And I think to myself,
Are all of them at fault,
Or is there something I lack?

The world is ending
So I'd better let you know-
I love you enough
To let you go.

41. Enamoured

I know these lines
Don't matter as much.
A billion different words
Won't make you love me as such.
And I know if you leave,
Nothing could make you stay,
So I put you into letters
To hold you close when you're away.

I know these lines
Don't matter as much.
Dreams might come true,
But you're the only reality I can't touch.

42. Jamais Vu

Just break my heart and go
Don't make it any worse
 Than it already is.
If you want me, let me know-
Don't make it any harder
Than it already is.

These feelings, I've felt before.
These patterns are all I've ever known.
Lived my life on bits and pieces
Of whatever the world had thrown.
People who were supposed to love me
Taught me how to live on my own.

43. Forever, Somewhere

If the multiverse does exist
I hope I found you
And as a matter of fact,
I know we are bound to-
See the worst in each other
And still be together.
Maybe in another universe
I'd hold you forever.

44. La Vida Es Hermosa Contigo

Wish I could leave you
All by yourself in this cruel world,
But it would be a sin.
The fear that you'll lose
Whatever little is left in you,
Always crawls under my skin.

And I can't let that happen, can I?
Your pain will be the death of me.
I love you enough for the both of us-
You've put your faith in me,
And I'll keep my faith in God,
As long as you're happy.

45. Redamancy

People say the love you give
Finds a way back to you.
I thought it was such bullshit-
Until the day I found you.

The day I felt the wind,
Brushing against my skin.
The day I felt these tears,
Washing away my sins.

The day the sun
Couldn't have shined brighter,
And the heart I carried
Had never felt lighter.

The day that never turned into night,
The day I could finally see the light.
The day I realised
We were meant to be-
Was the day I found love
That was made for me.

46. Yuanfen

Love doesn't do justice
To the feelings I have for you,
'Cause these four letters
Could never be enough for you.

So I let them flow through my veins,
Living in me like some kind of parasite-
Sometimes bleeding onto pages,
Manifesting into everything I write.

And if you start adding up the pieces,
You'll know this isn't love-
Never was. But so much more.
Something you've known to exist
But never experienced before.

47. Reverie

I've been sleeping a lot lately
'Cause that's the only time I can meet you.
Can't keep you out of my dreams,
'Cause that's the only place I can greet you.

And if you're all I have,
How the fuck could I mistreat you?
In a game I want you to win-
How could I ever defeat you?

Even if you're missing a piece,
I'm here to love the incomplete you.
And if all my memories blur
Of the days that precede you,
Or if this love is the end of us,
Just know that I want you-
More than I need you.

48. Cafuné

I envy the sun
Whose light gets to touch you,
Every morning as you wake up.
I envy the moon,
Peeking through your window
As you lie, without any makeup.

I envy the wind,
Caressing your skin,
Messing your hair.
I envy the winters
Feeling the warmth of your body-
Shivering in crisp, cold air.

I envy the earth,
Holding you so close,
While I don't even get to see you.
Is this the life I chose?

49. Meliorism

The world's a beautiful place
Because you exist in it.
My heart knows love,
Because you still persist in it.

Just like you do in every little thing
That surrounds me,
Constantly reminding me of your existence
When you're not around me.

But I hope it stays the same
Until one of us dies.
'Cause the world's a beautiful place
Until our hearts synchronize.

50. Sleepless Nights

I should've slept that night
When you needed me.
Maybe then you'd understand,
How it all feels.
Now I'm crying myself to sleep,
Over something even time won't heal.

And I should've walked away,
Instead of comforting you.
But how could I be
The one that's hurting you?

I should've slept that night-
But I chose to call you,
When every atom of my body
Was starting to fall for you.

51. Absquatulate

I'll never be enough for you
No matter how hard I try.
Only make life tough for you,
Always be the reason you cry.

But if-only if- you had known
All the efforts I made,
Beyond the ones that were shown,
Maybe you would've been kinder to me.

If only you'd forgiven my sins,
Instead of burning down my wings,
I might've been kinder to you.
But now, all we do is sigh,
Trying to find the good in goodbye.

52. Dreamscape

As soon as I close my eyes,
I could be anywhere I desire-
Could light up the nights
By setting skies on fire.

But every time I close my eyes,
All I see is you.
Staring through your honey-brown eyes
As your fingertips tuck your hair
Behind your ears.
While I stand there,
Holding back my tears.

You smile as you turn red,
Your lips crawling up your cheek.
And I realize- the reason for my strength
Also makes me weak.

And I find you in places
Unknown to me, yet still my favourites,
Just because you're there.
And now I don't want to wake up
With you not here.

So, I guess I'll stay with you-
Stay through lows and highs,
And live forever within limited time,
As long as I close my eyes.

53. Dum Spiro, Spero

I can't see you anymore
But your presence, I feel.
It's the body that's mine,
But the senses you steal.

I can't touch you anymore,
But you've touched my soul.
Been living my life in half-
It's after you that I'm whole.

I can't carry you anymore
In my heart, you'll always remain.
You're not dirt that wipes off easy,
You're blood, that leaves a stain.

54. Serein

Sometimes I imagine myself
In a world beside you,
Where I could touch you-
For real.

Trace my thumb
Along the outline of your smile,
Or the bulge of your veins
As your fingers interlock with mine.

Kiss your forehead-
One on each temple,
Gently rub your ears
When they turn red-hot
From the direct sunlight.

Tuck your hair behind them
On a windy day- or even
Smudge that teardrop
Off your cheek
On days when you can't.

55. Querencia

I know I hurt you,
I know I caused you pain.
But what good is a monsoon
Without a little rain?

I know you expect me to be perfect.
But I'm nowhere near.
I know you'll see it one day-
And it'll all be clear.

That my love for you
Is the purest there could be,
'Cause there will always be more
Than your eyes can see.

I know I hurt you,
And saying "I love you"
Will never be enough,
'Cause those three little words
Can never describe my love.

56. Habromania

I know we're not the same
And I don't expect you to be,
But when you say *"I love you"*
I just want you to see-
The one you love isn't me,
Just a mere reflection in your eye.
That's why you want me to be perfect,
While your expectations touch the sky.

And when reality comes crashing down,
I know you'll hate me eventually,
'Cause the version you fell for-
Isn't me, actually.

57. Chiaroscuro

I'm a different person around you,
And that's where the problem starts.
Why can't i be normal around you?
What if my feelings are pure-
Would you accept me for who I am,
Or would you not love me anymore?

Would you still want me
If I were honest with you?
Or would you rather prefer lies
And believe them to be true?

But most importantly
Would you stay
If I say I need you?
Or would you use it against me,
And make me regret it too?

58. Apricity

Love always finds a way-
At least, that is what people say.
But I never believed any of that,
Until I met you,
Like a long-lost dream
That finally came true.

Day by day,
We drifted apart-
Only by distance, never in heart.
Until one day, you broke the silence,
Broke your walls and pulled me close,
Lifted me up to safer grounds,
Away from all the highs and lows.

Away from all the pain and lies,
I found my peace in your eyes,
And my happiness in your smile
Pushes me to go the extra mile-
Just to make you stay for a while.

So take my hand, hold it tight,
Be my queen and I'll be your knight
I know it's hard, but we just might
Find our way back to light.

59. Aphelion

We were too good to be true
Maybe that's the reason
Why me and you
Pretended to ignore
What we could become-
Left our ships on shore
And never looked back at the sea,
Until we found our way
Back to each other
Like a lost kid,
Sensing his mother

But this time
We aren't afraid anymore
With our fingers intertwined
We left the shore
For the deep blue sea
That always hid
The love for you and me.

So hold your breath
And jump overboard-
Losing you again
Is something I can't afford.

Just hold my hand,
And we'll find a way.
Darling, it's time to live...
We'll die another day.

60. Sanctuary

When you're tired of your life,
And nothing feels quite right,
Come to me.

On days when you're guilty
Instead of staying up till three-
Come to me.

Even in times when you want to die,
But all you need is a shoulder to cry-
Come to me.

Come to me like a place,
You go, when you have things to share.
And even if God
Hasn't answered your prayer,
I'll suffer with you, gladly-
In times of despair.

61. Phosphenes

Of all the things I told you,
Half of them were lies–
'Cause when you said loving you was a sin,
I knew I'd do it twice.

Never even got a chance to say
How much you matter to me.
Instead, I lied to you,
So you'd never get to see

The things I hide, the feelings I conceal
Just to save you from myself–
'Cause I know how it feels
To be in love, but not be loved.

And I'm sorry if I hurt you
Or even pushed you aside.
If I ever say I hate you,
Just know that I lied.

62. Ataraxia

I hope death arrives
Uninvited, on a Sunday afternoon
With curtains drawn,
And a single ray of light
Stirring dust particles across the room.

I hope death arrives
A bit late than soon
Drunk and dazed,
As I lie there, next to you.